ॐ

GURU PUJA
THE DIVINE INVOCATION

Essence and Sanskrit Grammar

Ashwini Kumar Aggarwal

जय गुरुदेव

ISBN13: 978-93-95766-29-6 Paperback Edition
ISBN13: 978-93-95766-28-9 Hardbound Edition
ISBN13: 978-93-95766-31-9 Digital Edition

Title: **Guru Puja the Divine Invocation**
SubTitle: **Essence and Sanskrit Grammar**
Author: **Ashwini Kumar Aggarwal**

Printed and Published by
Devotees of Sri Sri Ravi Shankar Ashram
34 Sunny Enclave, Devigarh Road,
Patiala 147001, Punjab, India

https://advaita56.weebly.com/
The Art of Living Centre

https://www.artofliving.org/

28th Dec 2022, Sunview Residency Foundation with Sukhmani Sahib path & Joginder Singh Riar's kirtan. Pausha Shukla Shashti, Shatabhisha Nakshatra.
On this day in 1885 Indian National Congress founded at Gokuldas Tejpal Sanskrit College, 1895 Wilhelm Rontgen publishes X-ray paper, 1895 Birth of cinema by Lumiere brothers' film screening.
Vikram Samvat 2079 Nala, Saka Era 1944 Shubhakrit

1st Edition December 2022

जय गुरुदेव

Dedication

Sri Sri Ravi Shankar

who taught us divine worship via **'Bhanu didi'** and graced our course and told us the modified word त्रिगुणसहितम् to be chanted in live Guru's presence, VM Ground Floor, Navratri Oct 2011, Bangalore Ashram

Acknowledgements

Sukhmani Sahib Path at Sunview Residency (near NE Guru Sthana point), 10:30 to 11:45am, then soul stirring kirtan by Bhai Joginder Singh Riar till 12:30pm, followed by sumptuous langar.

- to honor human birth
- to engineer creativity
- to produce high performing individuals
- to help families live in close knit societies
- to enable man's inter-galactic travel
- to ignite love
- to spark devotion
- to kindle authenticity
- to rise above physics and
- play soccer with the nebulae

Front Cover Photo Courtesy

Marble inlay work at The Oberoi hotel, Marine Drive, Bombay. Photo by Ashwini.

Blessing

Guru Puja is the mother of all mantras, the maha mantra. You can make your whole body in such a way where it becomes an invitation to the Divine.

Guru Puja is an ancient Sanskrit invocation, which invites the ascended and enlightened masters to enter your space. The way the mantra is stated, there is no choice but for these Divine energies to answer the call of Guru Puja. As you give yourself to the process of this invocation, your energy aligns with the Divine.

Practicing Guru Puja on a regular basis will bring a different quality to your life. It awakens your inner divinity, allowing you to access peaceful and blissful feelings throughout your day. It is a powerful tool used by many yoga practitioners.

A Sanskrit chant with thirty six verses, within this mantra there are 16 ways in which we invoke the divine through powerful ceremony and ritual. It is a way to consecrate sacred space in your environment, your home, and around your sacred alter.

Sri Sri Ravi Shankar

Preface

Etymology and Essence

What is Puja?
Panini Dhatupatha Root 1642 पूज पूजायाम् । to worship.
पूजा = पूर्णात् जायते इति पूजा = that which is born of fullness is called Puja.
Fullness = a state of being satiated. A state of feeling wonderful within. Being grateful.

What is Guru?
गुरु = ग कु उच्च Panini Unadi Sutras 1.24 कृग्रोरुच्च e.g.
Root 1409 कॄ विक्षेपे । to scatter. किरति विक्षिपति शत्रून् इति कुरुः राजा । one who clears away enemies = kuru, king.
Root 1410 गॄ निगरणे । to swallow. गिरति इति गुरुः आचार्यः । one who clears doubts = guru, preceptor.

गु = something heavy, dense, gross, darkness or unfathomable, beyond reach, beyond the intellect.
रु = to throw light, illumine, carry easily, the state of being free from mine-ness or concepts.

Contents

BLESSING 5

PREFACE 6

PRAYER 9

PROLOGUE 10

VERSE 1 HALLOWED LINEAGE 12

MAKING IT PURE FEARLESS SHIELDED 14

INVOKING THE DIVINE 18

How this Consciousness Manifests 18
Personal Ancestral Role 24
Faculty and Scriptures that nourish Soul 28
Erudite Scholar Exemplary Teacher 32
Makes me thoroughly Satiated............................34
I Meditate upon the Light....................................36

THE SIXTEEN OFFERINGS IN PUJA 38

1st Proper Welcome..38
2nd Exalted Seat..40
3rd Use of Wash and Bath facility.........................42
4th Be properly dressed for the Occasion 44
5th Bring the Mind to the Present Moment...........46
6th Praise for the sacrosanct occasion 48
7th Fragile Delicate Momentary 50
8th Shield Cover the Precious...............................52
9th Lamp Light spreads far and wide.....................54
10th Water is Love that flows deep inside 56
11th Hearty Meal celebrates togetherness 58
12th Enjoyable Drink to cement the Union 60
13th Strength check and restore...........................62
14th Humility preserve 64

AARTI - LAMPS **66**

15th Offer Everything *68*
Offer Intimacy *68*

GRATEFULNESS – FLOWERS **70**

Acknowledge the Space *72*
Acknowledge the Wisdom *74*
Acknowledge the Purity *76*
Acknowledge the Body *78*
16th Drop yourSelf *80*

SILENCE **82**

BHAJAN – SINGING **83**

LATIN TRANSLITERATION CHART **85**

VERSES FOR CHANTING **86**

SANSKRIT GRAMMAR **92**

CONJUGATION PROCESS OF VERB **95**

DECLENSION PROCESS OF NOUN **96**

CLASS NOTES **97**

REFERENCES **99**

EPILOGUE **100**

Prayer

त्वमेव माता च पिता त्वमेव
त्वमेव बन्धुश्च सखा त्वमेव ।
त्वमेव विद्या द्रविणं त्वमेव
त्वमेव सर्वं मम देवदेव ॥

tvameva mātā ca pitā tvameva
tvameva bandhuśca sakhā tvameva I
tvameva vidyā draviṇaṃ tvameva ,
tvameva sarvaṃ mama devadeva II

Thee indeed alone are my loving Mother and protective Father.
Thee indeed alone are my caring Relation and trusted Friend.
Thee indeed alone are my true Education and total Bank balance.
Thee indeed alone are All, my Lord and Master.

Prologue

Prior to the actual Puja, while things are being arranged, and people are still coming in, we do:

- Nadi Shodhan Pranayama
- Group chanting e.g., slow Om Namah Shivaya

We also ensure there is:

- Someone to welcome the attendee
- Another to apply chandan tilak
- Someone to guide them to the seat or wash

Additionally, we see there is

- Someone to take calls regarding directions to the venue or any other queries
- Someone to help in parking

Verse 1 Hallowed Lineage

<u>गुरु परम्परा स्तोत्रम्</u>

सदाशिवसमारम्भां शङ्कराचार्यमध्यमाम् ।

अस्मद् श्रीगुरुपर्यन्तां वन्दे गुरुपरम्पराम् ॥ १

<u>guru paramparā stotram</u>

sadāśivasamārambhāṃ śaṅkarācāryamadhyamām ।

asmad śrīguruparyantāṃ vande guruparamparām ॥ 1

सदाशिवसमारम्भाम् शङ्कराचार्यमध्यमाम् ।

अस्मत् श्रीगुरुपर्यन्ताम् वन्दे गुरुपरम्पराम् ॥

सदा-शिव-सम्-आरम्भाम् [f2/1] that tradition which has perfectlyEvolved from the eternalLordShiva शङ्कराचार्य-मध्यमाम् [f2/1] the tradition that has Adi Shankaracharya somewhere in between । अस्मत् [mfn5/3] from our श्री-गुरु-पर्यन्ताम् [m6/3] extending till our current exalted Master वन्दे [लट् i/1] I salute गुरु-परम्पराम् [m6/3] tradition of sacred Masters ॥

वन्दे from Dhatupatha 11. वन्द् अभिवादनस्तुत्योः । 1cA

1.

It feels so good to trace and acknowledge my divine ancestry and rich lineage.

In India, we always think of Lord Shiva as our primordal father. He is our first teacher. He is eternally present with us.

Lord Shiva → Adi Shankaracharya → current preceptor (Sri Sri Ravi Shankar).

A beautiful statement, wherein we bring to mind our present Master, and endow him with all qualities of

- Adi Shankaracharya (a historical personage), and
- The eternal Lord Shiva

Lord Shiva is stated as "eternal", i.e., ever present in life, always available in any given moment.

Adi Shankaracharya is the supreme teacher of life, who taught practically each man, woman, and child; in person.

Making it Pure Fearless Shielded

<u>पवित्रीकरणं मन्त्रम्</u>

अपवित्रः पवित्रो वा सर्वावस्थाङ्गतोऽपि वा ।

यस्स्मरेत् पुण्डरीकाक्षं स बाह्याभ्यन्तरः शुचिः ॥ २

<u>pavitrīkaraṇam mantram</u>

apavitraḥ pavitro vā sarvāvasthāṅgato'pi vā ।

yassmaret puṇḍarīkākṣaṃ sa bāhyābhyantaraḥ śuciḥ ॥ 2

अपवित्रः पवित्रः वा सर्वावस्थाम् गतः अपि वा ।

यः स्मरेत् पुण्डरीकाक्षम् सः बाह्याभ्यन्तरः शुचिः ॥

अ-पवित्रः [m1/1] un-clean पवित्रः [m1/1] clean वा [0] or सर्व-अवस्थाम् [f2/1] any-situation गतः [PPP क्त m1/1] occurred अपि [0] also वा [0] or । यः [m1/1] whosoever स्मरेत् [विलि॰ iii/1] shall remember पुण्डरीकाक्षम् [m2/1] lotus-eyed Lord Vishnu सः [m1/1] he बाह्य-आभ्यन्तरः [m1/1] outer-inner शुचिः [m1/1] purity (shall attain) ॥

स्मरेत् from 933. स्मृ चिन्तायाम् । 1cP

2.

What is dirt and what is cleanliness? Is it of the body? Or is it regarding the mind and thinking? My lord who is in the form of my Guru, i seek your guidance in this regard. Please enlighten me, beloved Master.

So saying as i submit in graceful surrender, it flashes...

It is of the place, it is of the ambience, it is of the people i am with, it is of the people on the fringe. Dirt and Cleanliness are multidimensional and extend far beyond my clothes, my body, my thoughts and decision making.

How i spend my time, where i visit, whom i meet, and the aura and ambience of the immediate locality as well as the distant surroundings, the season and climate, all of it has a big role.

Dirt or Cleanliness. Which do i prefer? Which do i encourage? What are my views and personal opinions? What is my inner code of conduct?

Does a muddy face, torn shoes, soiled clothes and general aura of lacking money invoke within a revolting sense of dirt?

or Does a rich attire that arouses lust and expensive car with a liquor bottle, cigar in hand, mouthing expletives, make me feel any Cleanliness?

Where am i? Where do i stand? With whom shall i while my time and whom shall i befriend?

At the onset i pose this Q to my Master. I seek his help in this matter so that my time on planet Earth may be fruitful and to my liking.

What is Dirt? What is Cleanliness? My dear Lord kindly enlighten...

The answer is not long in coming. However it is so thick and deep and heavy that i must sit down and become comfortable first. I must take a good shower and change my clothes. I must do some stretches and deep breathing and become relaxed so that i can understand and accept the answer.

Bit by bit it dawns. Slowly it opens.

Whether unclean or clean it matters not. Place or season has nothing to do. People or ambience have little say.

Have your focus on the Divine. Keep your crosshair on the Lord. Wish the Lord, want the Divine, have Him alone in your sight.

And the world will turn for you.

Go O go,

make your decisions,
take your chances,
follow them through,

And the world **will turn** for you.

How this Consciousness Manifests

<u>आवाहनम्</u>

नारायणं पद्मभवं वशिष्ठं शक्तिञ्च तत्पुत्रपराशरञ्च ।
व्यासं शुकं गौडपदं महान्तं गोविन्दयोगीन्द्रमथास्य शिष्यम् ॥ ३

<u>āvāhanam</u>

nārāyaṇaṃ padmabhavaṃ vaśiṣṭhaṃ śaktiñca tatputraparāśarañca I vyāsaṃ śukaṃ gauḍapadaṃ mahāntaṃ govindayogīndramathāsya śiṣyam II 3

नारायणम् पद्मभवम् वशिष्ठम् शक्तिम् च तत्पुत्रपराशरम् च ।
व्यासम् शुकम् गौडपदम् महान्तम् गोविन्दयोगीन्द्रम् अथ अस्य शिष्यम् ॥

नारायणम् $^{m2/1}$ to Narayana पद्मभवम् $^{m2/1}$ to LotusNavelBorn i.e. Brahma वशिष्ठम् $^{m2/1}$ to Vasistha शक्तिम् $^{m2/1}$ to Shakti च ^{0} and तत्पुत्र-पराशरम् $^{m2/1}$ to that son (each of successive); Parashara च ^{0} and । व्यासम् $^{m2/1}$ to Vyasa शुकम् $^{m2/1}$ to Shuka गौडपदम् $^{m2/1}$ to Gaudapada महान्तम् $^{m2/1\ adj}$ great गोविन्द-योगीन्द्रम् $^{m2/1}$ to the protector and uniter i.e. Govind Yogindra अथ ^{0} now अस्य$^{m6/1}$ of his शिष्यम् $^{m2/1}$ disciple ॥

3.

Having made this wonderful decision, i relax, i smile, and then i make arrangements to welcome the Divine.

Now who or what do i welcome?

Narayana - one like the pure water flow which gives peace and pleasantness immediately.

Of Narayana is born Padmabhava. Or, Narayana's best pupil, foremost disciple.

Padmabhava - one so tender like a fresh lotus, or, one born from the lotus-like navel of the galaxy. One who is like fresh churned butter. So heavenly. Both centripetal and centrifugal forces working in tandem result in a top-notch product, this physics is hinted here.

Of Padmabhava is born Vasistha. Or, Padmabhava's best pupil, foremost disciple.

Vasistha - the one established in excellence. The one whose decisions are precise, pragmatic, and yield immediate as well as long term gains.

Of Vasistha is born Shakti. Or, brilliant decisions lead to bubbling energy and banish all fatigue.

Shakti - the embodiment of energy. Always enthusiastic, with limitless endurance, and having superhuman force.

Of Shakti is born Parashara. Or, the beginning of time and space. From the big bang was born this visible creation infused with consciousness.

Parashara - the ageless, the one whose starting point cannot be precisely determined, the one with complete knowledge of stars and planets, galaxies, and their movements and influences and effects.

Of Parashara is born Vyasa. Or, the distinction between truth and untruth, the duality, the transcendental and the transactional creation.

Vyasa - the giver of duality, the enforcer of balance, the separator of strength and weakness. That from whom we get the discrimination faculty. That due to whom the creation gets 'opposite values', the reason why good and bad stand equal in strength, moreover either deserves respect and both must be present in life. The combination of Sattva Rajas Tamas is made and its harmony is necessary in life.

Of Vyasa is born Shuka. Or, the graceful truth.

Shuka - Truth may be dry and cutting or healing and satisfying. Shuka is the truth that pleases as well as cures, revives the senses and infuses love and gratefulness.

By Shuka is nurtured Gaudapada. Or, during upbringing and raising a child, the essential and most significant quality is being loving and truthful. Speaking the truth with sweetness. Blending discipline with self-effacement.

Gaudapada - the origin of Advaita Vedanta. The starting point of turning the senses inwards and being absorbed in the inner blissful pure ecstasy. Self-enquiry now begins and it is called Mahanta, the ultimate vocation.

From this point onwards, the discrimination regarding the highest is first established with utmost clarity. Who is the Supreme? Who is God? What is that which is to be revered and aimed for? Gaudapada states it is something within. The inner space in each one is God. The innermost of all things is God. Training the mind bit by bit to go inwards leads to freedom from misery. It is the path of enlightenment.

By Gaudapada is deeply influenced Govind Yogindra. Or, when the inner journey begins, one gets to see what is also needed in the outer, and one begins to formulate concrete steps that will support and enhance the path to Divinity.

Govind Yogindra - the one who embraces divinity and follows the quintessential principles of

- Govind = watch over senses and proper and balanced use of senses, including keeping them bright and sharp, by the principles of Yoga-Indriya.
- Yoga = a perfect mix of Meditation, Hard work, truthful speech. Union of body breath thought emotion.

Having a reverence for life and matter, expressing oneself to one's full potential. Caring for oneself and caring for the planet. Forgiving oneself and remaining lighthearted and cheerful.

Govind Yogindra finds and perfects his direct disciple **Adi Shankaracharya**, Or when a Guru manifests, a sincere devotee gets born to illumine his teachings, open them to the world in large in a manner the world can accept and digest.

E.g.

Krishna → Arjuna,

Ashtavakra → Janaka,

Ramakrishna Paramahamsa → Vivekananda,

Aurobindo → Mother Mirra,

Yukteshwar Giri → Paramahamsa Yogananda

Brahmananda Saraswati → Sri Sri Ravi Shankar.

Personal Ancestral Role

श्री शङ्कराचार्यमथास्य पद्मपादञ्च हस्तामलकञ्च शिष्यम् ।
तं त्रोटकं वार्त्तिककारमन्यान् अस्मद् गुरून् सन्ततमानतोऽस्मि ॥
४

śrī śaṅkarācāryamathāsya padmapādañca hastāmalakañca śiṣyam | taṃ troṭakaṃ vārttikakāramanyān asmad gurūn santatamānato'smi ||
4

श्री शङ्कराचार्यम् अथ अस्य पद्मपादम् च हस्तामलकम् च शिष्यम् । तम् त्रोटकम् वार्त्तिककारम् अन्यान् अस्मत् गुरून् सन्ततमानतः अस्मि ॥

श्री [0] honorable शङ्कराचार्यम् [m2/1] Adi Shankaracharya अथ [0] now अस्य [m6/1] of his पद्म-पादम् [m2/1] lotusFeet i.e. Padmapada च [0] and हस्त-अमलकम् [m2/1] crystal clear as a gooseberry on one's palm i.e. Hastamalaka च [0] and शिष्यम् [m2/1] disciple । तम् [m2/1] him त्रोटकम् [m2/1] Trotaka वार्त्तिक-कारम् [m2/1] commentary (Vartika) writer i.e. Sureshvara अन्यान् [m2/3] others अस्मत् [m5/3] from our गुरून् [m2/3] masters सन्तत-मानतः [0] continuousSeries-honorable अस्मि [लट् i/1] I am (invoking welcoming prayerfully) ॥

The 4 disciples of Adi Shankara पद्मपाद , हस्तामलक , त्रोटक , वार्तिककार सुरेश्वर ।

अस्मि from 1065. अस् भुवि । 2cP

4.

Adi Shankaracharya - the boy who attained enlightenment at the age of 8. The Avatar who joined hearts, fused practices, melded minds, and established the foundation of all wisdom seen and practiced currently in the world. The one who travelled the length and breadth of India twice and met almost the entire populace personally; a feat still unequalled and unparalleled. Even though we have fast cars and airplanes, even though we have phone and messenger and chat. The man with the largest and most courageous heart and perfect perception in the history of planet Earth.

The four directions came to sit and learn at the feet of the great Master. Men who were already enlightened, perfected siddhas with many talents and virtues, came humbly to serve and partake of the company of Adi Shankara. Shankara lit the beacon of divine purpose in every heart, he dusted away the incorrigible layers of flimsy notions concepts beliefs, and firmly established Advaita Vedanta on planet Earth. He resuscitated the Sanatana mindset, and opened the gates to freedom for all of mankind.

East	Puri	Padmapada	Rigveda
West	Dwarka	Hastamalaka	Samaveda
North	Joshimath	Trotakacharya	Atharvaveda
South	Shringeri	Sureshvaracharya	Yajurveda

East	Rigveda	the cosmic laws and natural forces
West	Samaveda	the sounds, music, and harmony in creation
North	Atharvaveda	the definitive guide for units, individuals, humans, basic elements and entities
South	Yajurveda	the injuncts for society, school, organization, city, country to function

We welcome the blend of

- independence and interdependence,

and the sublime forces which keep us

- apart and distinct;

at the same time

- united and one.

Faculty and Scriptures that nourish Soul

श्रुतिस्मृतिपुराणानाम् आलयं करुणालयम् ।
नमामि भगवत्पादं शङ्करं लोकशङ्करम् ॥ ५

śrutismṛtipurāṇānām ālayaṃ karuṇālayam ।
namāmi bhagavatpādaṃ śaṅkaraṃ lokaśaṅkaram ॥ 5

श्रुतिस्मृतिपुराणानाम् आलयम् करुणालयम् ।
नमामि भगवत्पादम् शङ्करम् लोकशङ्करम् ॥

श्रुति-स्मृति-पुराणानाम् $^{n6/3}$ of that heard-remembered-culturalValueBasedReporting आलयम् $^{n2/1}$ a covered area करुणा-आलयम् $^{n2/1\ adj}$ an abode of compassion । नमामि $^{\text{लट्}\ i/1}$ I bow भगवत्-पादम् $^{m2/1\ adj}$ शङ्करम् $^{m2/1}$ to the one having illustrious Feet and giver of bliss i.e. Adi Shankaracharya लोक-शङ्करम् $^{m2/1}$ to emancipator of the world ॥

नमामि from 981. नम् प्रह्वत्वे शब्दे च ।

5.

We also welcome the faculty of hearing or Shruti - that which goes into the intellect undiluted and causes a

- resurgence of cognition,
- recognition,
- change in will,
- change in values,
- change in perception,
- change in opinion.

We welcome the faculty of remembrance or Smriti - that which holds the sum total of our sojourn of 400 years,

- where each breath and moment get printed,
- where each person and event gets recorded,
- where our talents, limits, limitations and intentions are carefully indexed.

Smriti is also called Citta, the end-to-end container of time's arrow.

40% content is personal, wakeful, alert, conscious. The rest 60% is external, cosmic, beyond time-space-consciousness, the unknown, unexplained, unexperienced.

And then we welcome the Purana, literature that is a mix of history, geography, culture, and value system, and so fantastically written that it feels it applies to our own life right here and now. Ever new, applicable to most of the situations and places on planet Earth in real time.

List of 18 Mahapurana

Agni Purana अग्नि पुराण	Bhagavata Purana भागवत महापुराण	Bhavishya Purana भविष्य पुराण
Brahma Purana ब्रह्म पुराण	Brahma Vaivarta Purana ब्रह्म वैवर्त पुराण	Brahmanda Purana ब्रह्माण्ड पुराण
Garuda Purana गरुड़ पुराण	Kurma Purana कूर्म पुराण	Linga Purana लिङ्ग पुराण
Markandeya Purana मार्कण्डेय पुराण	Matsya Purana मत्स्य पुराण	Narada Purana नारद पुराण
Padma Purana पद्म पुराण	Shiva Purana शिव पुराण	Skanda Purana स्कन्द पुराण
Vamana Purana वामन पुराण	Varaha Purana वाराह पुराण	Vishnu Purana विष्णु पुराण

There are also 18 Upapurana.

We welcome all abodes and places, treating them as an outpouring of the Lord's kindness. Know that whether it is our home, or office, or vehicle, or hotel, or park or shopping center, each is infused with the Lord's benign presence, and each is worthy of honor and respect.

We again reiterate our welcome to Adi Shankaracharya, who is the giver of complete education.

He reached out to each and everyone in the countryside, he interfaced with men, women and children, he taught the dinacharya and the rituals and practices, he taught how to celebrate festivals and events.

He established the code of conduct, the Yama and Niyama. He restored the sanctity of relationships and enforced the value system and discipline in society.

Erudite Scholar Exemplary Teacher

शङ्करं शङ्कराचार्यं केशवं बादरायणम् ।
सूत्रभाष्यकृतौ वन्दे भगवन्तौ पुनᳶ पुनः ॥ ६

śaṅkaraṃ śaṅkarācāryaṃ keśavaṃ bādarāyaṇam ।
sūtrabhāṣyakṛtau vande bhagavantau puna× punaḥ ॥ 6

शङ्करम् शङ्कराचार्यम् केशवम् बादरायणम् ।
सूत्रभाष्यकृतौ वन्दे भगवन्तौ पुनः पुनः ॥

शङ्करम् m2/1 adj **शङ्कराचार्यम्** m2/1 to bliss giver Adi Shankaracharya **केशवम्** m2/1 adj **बादरायणम्** m2/1 to Keshava Badarayana i.e. Vyasa । **सूत्र-भाष्य-कृतौ** m2/2 to scripters of Sutras and Bhashya **वन्दे** लट् i/1 I salute **भगवन्तौ** m2/2 to the illustrious duo **पुनः** 0 adv again and **पुनः** 0 adv again ॥

6.

Now we invoke the duo of Adi Shankara and Veda Vyasa.

Vyasa is famous as the author of the Mahabharata. He is also responsible for classifying the Vedas into distinct texts, and making a list of all available literature in systematic manner.

Vyasa is the rishi by whose grace Pandu and Dhritarashtra were born, or the birth of opposing forces.

Vyasa wrote the analytic Vedantic text known as the Brahma Sutras, of **Prasthanatrayi** fame, viz. Upanishads, Bhagavad Gita, Brahma Sutras.

Adi Shankaracharya wrote a Bhashya or detailed commentary or gloss on eleven Upanishads, the Bhagavad Gita and the Brahma Sutras.

We are not simply remembering Vyasa and Adi Shankara, but we are calling to mind the faculty of writing, discussing, and elucidating upon wisdom. Wisdom is the practical aspect of living life, and the works on wisdom give us insights on how to go about situations and events in a successful manner.

Makes me thoroughly Satiated

यद्द्वारे निखिला निलिम्पपरिषद् सिद्धिं विधत्तेऽनिशम् ।
श्रीमच्छ्रीलसितं जगद्गुरुपदं नत्वात्मतृप्तिङ्गताः ॥ ७

yaddvāre nikhilā nilimpapariṣad siddhiṃ vidhatte'niśam
| śrīmacchrīlasitaṃ jagadgurupadaṃ
natvātmatṛptiṅgatāḥ || 7

यत् द्वारे निखिला निलिम्पपरिषद् सिद्धिम् विधत्ते अनिशम् ।
श्रीमत् श्रीलसितम् जगद्गुरुपदम् नत्वा आत्मतृप्तिम् गताः ॥

यत् n2/1 whose द्वारे n7/1 at the door निखिला f1/1 entire निलिम्पपरिषद् f1/1 galaxy of divine souls सिद्धिम् f2/1 perfection विधत्ते लट् iii/1 render support अनिशम् f2/1 incessant । श्रीमत् n2/1 to splendorous श्रीलसितम् n2/1 to glorious play जगत्-गुरु-पदम् n2/1 to planet preceptor's word नत्वा त्वा 0 gerund having bowed आत्म-तृप्तिम् f2/1 soul satiated गताः क्त m1/3 PPP *all* become ॥

विधत्ते from वि + 1092. डुधाञ् धारणपोषणयोः । 3cU.
विधत्ते + अनिशम् → 6.1.109 एङः पदान्तादति । पूर्वरूप सन्धिः → विधत्तेऽनिशम् ।

7.

We give profuse praises to the assembled divinities, especially to our Guru's preceptor.

We sing superlative glories. We say that our Guru has been instructed by the one at whose door the entire galaxy of gods waits upon continuously, seeking perfection, and rendering special support.

He has effulgent intellect, his deeds are brilliant, he is the teacher of the entire world.

Having bowed down at the heavenly feet of such a divine soul, our own soul tastes the nectar of bliss.

We all become colored by his vision, we all get soaked in his charm, and we all attain to great heights.

I Meditate upon the Light

लोकाज्ञानपयोदपाटनधुरं श्री शङ्करं शर्मदम् ।
ब्रह्मानन्दसरस्वतीं गुरुवरं ध्यायामि ज्योतिर्मयम् ॥ ८

lokājñānapayodapāṭhanadhuraṃ śrī śaṅkaraṃ śarmadam I brahmānandasarasvatīṃ guruvaraṃ dhyāyāmi jyotirmayam II 8

लोकाज्ञानपयोदपाटनधुरम् श्री शङ्करम् शर्मदम् ।
ब्रह्मानन्दसरस्वतीम् गुरुवरम् ध्यायामि ज्योतिः मयम् ॥

लोक-अज्ञान-पयोद-पाटन-धुरम् [m2/1] to the one who worldly ignorance *like* a cloud burst cleaves श्री [0] to the glorious (title) शङ्करम् [m2/1] to Shankara शर्मदम् [m2/1] to the prosperity maker । ब्रह्म-आनन्द-सरस्वतीम् [f2/1] to Brahman *like* happiness *that is* crystal clear गुरुवरम् [m2/1] to the one who banishes darkness ध्यायामि [लट् i/1] I meditate upon ज्योतिः [f1/1] the light मयम् [adj 2/1] *who is* made up of ॥

ध्यायामि from 908. ध्यै चिन्तायाम् । 1cP

8.

He is the one who rents asunder the cloud of doubt, despair, ignorance, indecision.

He is Shankara, the maker of prosperity. He just fashions wealth and resources and showers them upon us. He opens up our vision and makes us reach for the stars.

He is the one who radiates Brahmi happiness.
He totally banishes my gloom and depression.

I meditate upon Him.
I see Him as a loving glow.
To me He is light alone.

He is my path. My duty and my responsibility.

The Sixteen Offerings in Puja

1st Proper Welcome

षोडशोपचार पूजनम्

आवाहनं समर्पयामि श्रीगुरुचरणकमलेभ्यो नमः । १

ṣoḍaśopacāra pūjanam

āvāhanaṃ

samarpayāmi śrīgurucaraṇakamalebhyo namaḥ । 1

आवाहनम् समर्पयामि श्रीगुरुचरणकमलेभ्यः नमः ।

आवाहनम् $^{n2/1}$ Invocation, i.e. prayerful welcome समर्पयामि लट् $^{i/1}$ i heartily offer श्री-गुरु-चरण-कमलेभ्यः $^{m4/3}$ to exalted master's lotus-like feet नमः $^{n2/1}$ *as an act of my* humble obeisance

---

षोडशोपचार = षोडश उपचार = vowel sandhi अ+उ=ओ ।

समर्पयामि = 1st person present tense singular verb.

Root 936. ॠ गतिप्रापणयोः । णिजन्ते = अर्पय । अर्पयामि = लट् $^{i/1}$ । with upasarga सम् + अर्पयामि = समर्पयामि ।

नमः = 2nd case object, stem नमस् ^{n} ।

1.

The PUJA begins with a respectful and joyous welcoming.

A cheery hospitality with a red-carpet welcome sets the tone for us to feel a deep connect with the Divine Master.

The Master isn't looking for anything grand, at the same time a sense of admiration and belongingness from our side is being noticed by the subtle forces of Nature. These subtle energies then shower their appreciative blessings on all gathered for the Puja, especially on the yajaman or the host.

This is a prerequisite for the proceedings to begin favorably and usher great success.

श्रीगुरुचरणकमलेभ्यः = we offer it all at the feet of the Master. This symbolizes that the Master is the one who can go anywhere and do anything, hence his feet are to be worshipped so that they stay with us for a while…

Lotus-like feet, meaning that the feet which move in this world of harsh-muddy-thorny emotions and thoughts, yet remain soft-delicate-fragrant-handsome.

2nd Exalted Seat

आसनं समर्पयामि श्रीगुरुचरणकमलेभ्यो नमः । २

āsanaṃ

samarpayāmi śrīgurucaraṇakamalebhyo namaḥ । 2

आसनम् समर्पयामि श्रीगुरुचरणकमलेभ्यः नमः ।

आसनम् [n2/1] seat समर्पयामि [लट् i/1] i heartily offer श्री-गुरु-चरण-कमलेभ्यः [m4/3] to exalted master's lotus-like feet नमः [n2/1] humble obeisance

2.

After the warm welcome and pleasantries, we now usher in the Divine Master and show him his exalted seat.

A high seat is simply a symbol of flow, just as water flows from a higher level to the lower level, or energy flows from a higher voltage to the lower.

We must ensure that the Master's seat is properly made, it is clean and dry and comfortable to his liking.

A high seat doesn't necessarily mean raised, it simply means "to make the arrangements that are conducive and cherished by the Master". Not only regarding the seating; but the general ambience, lighting, temperature, decorations, all must be balanced, tasteful and befitting.

3rd Use of Wash and Bath facility

स्नानं समर्पयामि श्रीगुरुचरणकमलेभ्यो नमः । ३

snānaṃ

samarpayāmi śrīgurucaraṇakamalebhyo namaḥ । 3

स्नानम् समर्पयामि श्रीगुरुचरणकमलेभ्यः नमः ।

स्नानम् [n2/1] wash of mouth, hands, feet समर्पयामि [लट् i/1] i heartily offer श्री-गुरु-चरण-कमलेभ्यः [m4/3] to exalted master’s lotus-like feet नमः [n2/1] humble obeisance

3.

Water is life and life runs on water. A proper wash of face, hands and feet restores the humor of any traveler.

Use of bath facilities at onset relaxes the natural urges of the body, then the mind can be more available to the task at hand.

Wash and bath is mentioned to symbolize the purity and cleanliness of the proceedings, it is not necessarily a physical act.

Moreover any member of the congregation may wish to use such a facility, so it must be available during analogous occasions.

What we offer to the Master (or honored guest) is something that we also must imbibe and follow when we visit some place.

4th Be properly dressed for the Occasion

वस्त्रं समर्पयामि श्रीगुरुचरणकमलेभ्यो नमः । ४

vastraṃ

samarpayāmi śrīgurucaraṇakamalebhyo namaḥ । 4

वस्त्रम् समर्पयामि श्रीगुरुचरणकमलेभ्यः नमः ।

वस्त्रम् n2/1 spotless new cloth समर्पयामि लट् i/1 i heartily offer श्री-गुरु-चरण-कमलेभ्यः m4/3 to exalted master's lotus-like feet नमः n2/1 humble obeisance

4.

We offer the honored guest with a fresh cloth to wipe himself, we also offer him fresh clothes and attire as per his liking.

Wearing correct clothes and being properly dressed is a big boost to our ego and enhances our efficiency and performance.

For work or school wear the formal dress or uniform, for play wear the appropriate clothes and shoes, for sight-seeing and visiting see how the general folks are dressed.

For Sleep or Yoga or Meditation, see to it also.

Ensure the clothes are freshly washed, shoes and footwear are properly brushed. Torn or faded clothes may be repaired if possible or discarded. Neatness in grooming is advised.

5th Bring the Mind to the Present Moment

चन्दनं समर्पयामि श्रीगुरुचरणकमलेभ्यो नमः । ५

candanaṃ

samarpayāmi śrīgurucaraṇakamalebhyo namaḥ । 5

चन्दनम् समर्पयामि श्रीगुरुचरणकमलेभ्यः नमः ।

चन्दनम् [n2/1] sandalwood paste समर्पयामि [लट् i/1] i heartily offer श्री-गुरु-चरण-कमलेभ्यः [m4/3] to exalted master's lotus-like feet नमः [n2/1] humble obeisance

5.

When all have settled down and taken their seat, we begin the Puja by anointing sandalwood paste.

Sandalwood fragrance has been traditionally used to calm the mind, it is generally smeared on the third-eye in between the eyebrows.

This symbolizes that at the beginning of a task, we must become alert and aware of the situation and the people, and then act accordingly.

The third eye is the point where the pituitary and the pineal glands are situated an inch deeper inside.

These glands serve as the master control of the endocrine system, and many bodily activities are dependent on their smooth functioning.

Applying sandalwood paste at this point has a favorable impact on these glands, and thereby ensures our mind-body complex is ready for the present moment, and our intellect is cool and available to make correct decisions.

6th Praise for the sacrosanct occasion

अक्षतान् समर्पयामि श्रीगुरुचरणकमलेभ्यो नमः । ६
akṣatān
samarpayāmi śrīgurucaraṇakamalebhyo namaḥ । 6

अक्षतान् समर्पयामि श्रीगुरुचरणकमलेभ्यः नमः ।

अक्षतान् [m2/3] rice grains समर्पयामि [लट् i/1] i heartily offer श्री-गुरु-चरण-कमलेभ्यः [m4/3] to exalted master's lotus-like feet नमः [n2/1] humble obeisance

---

अक्षतान् from अ-क्षत = inviolable, unbroken, untampered, undecayed.

6.

Now we sprinkle white rice grains as an offering. Rice grains symbolize many things, amongst them some notable mentions:

- praise
- abundance
- wholeness
- complete
- fulsome
- purity
- divinity
- staple food item

Across many cultures and continents, rice is a staple diet and most loved foodgrain. Children especially enjoy rice dishes a lot.

It also gives a sense of wholeness i.e., new and unused, fresh and pure.

Sprinkling rice is an age-old custom to make the aura benign, by praising and nourishing the subtle and hidden energies.

7th Fragile Delicate Momentary

पुष्पं समर्पयामि श्रीगुरुचरणकमलेभ्यो नमः । ७

puṣpaṃ

samarpayāmi śrīgurucaraṇakamalebhyo namaḥ । 7

पुष्पम् समर्पयामि श्रीगुरुचरणकमलेभ्यः नमः ।

पुष्पम् $^{n2/1}$ flower समर्पयामि $^{\text{लट्}\ i/1}$ i heartily offer श्री-गुरु-चरण-कमलेभ्यः $^{m4/3}$ to exalted master's lotus-like feet नमः $^{n2/1}$ humble obeisance

7.

We gently place a delicate flower.

Flowers symbolize impermanence.

They symbolize softness, freshness, sweetness.

The multiple colors evoke acceptance, and make us properly responsive to difficult or unfavorable circumstances, also reminding us of their short span.

The various colors also give us choices in life, and alternate options to proceed gracefully in all matters.

8th Shield Cover the Precious

धूपं समर्पयामि श्रीगुरुचरणकमलेभ्यो नमः । ८
dhūpaṃ
samarpayāmi śrīgurucaraṇakamalebhyo namaḥ । 8

धूपम् समर्पयामि श्रीगुरुचरणकमलेभ्यः नमः ।

धूपम् n2/1 incense समर्पयामि लट् i/1 i heartily offer श्री-गुरु-चरण-कमलेभ्यः m4/3 to exalted master's lotus-like feet नमः n2/1 humble obeisance

8.

Aroma and smoke, both are used as a diversion and a cover in tactical operations.

Both fragrance and smoke cleanse the emotional aura and the physical bacteria.

The incense acts like a haze on the proceedings, shielding from prying eyes, and nosy customers.

Aroma is also used as a therapy to cure many ills.

9th Lamp Light spreads far and wide

दीपं समर्पयामि श्रीगुरुचरणकमलेभ्यो नमः । ९

dīpaṃ

samarpayāmi śrīgurucaraṇakamalebhyo namaḥ । 9

दीपम् समर्पयामि श्रीगुरुचरणकमलेभ्यः नमः ।

दीपम् n2/1 ghee lamp समर्पयामि लट् i/1 i heartily offer श्री-गुरु-चरण-कमलेभ्यः m4/3 to exalted master's lotus-like feet नमः n2/1 humble obeisance

9.

We light a lamp, the quality of the Fire Element. Light or Heat is given due regard in our life.

Light up the way,
Light up the morn,
Light up the aim,

Fire up the effort.

10th Water is Love that flows deep inside

आचमनीयं समर्पयामि श्रीगुरुचरणकमलेभ्यो नमः । १०

ācamanīyaṃ

samarpayāmi śrīgurucaraṇakamalebhyo namaḥ । 10

आचमनीयम् समर्पयामि श्रीगुरुचरणकमलेभ्यः नमः ।

आचमनीयम् [n2/1] drinking water समर्पयामि [लट् i/1] i heartily offer श्री-गुरु-चरण-कमलेभ्यः [m4/3] to exalted master's lotus-like feet नमः [n2/1] humble obeisance

10.

We sprinkle mineral water drops, the quality of the Water Element. Water or Love is given due regard in our life.

In the early days, our parents used to say “water is precious, close the taps properly after use”.

Water also represents the wealth in life. If there are leaky taps, for sure our money will not stay, the more we earn, the more shall we spend...

Water is the symbol of Love.
It is the symbol of Purity.
It helps engender Harmony.

11th Hearty Meal celebrates togetherness

नैवेद्यं समर्पयामि श्रीगुरुचरणकमलेभ्यो नमः । ११

naivedyaṃ

samarpayāmi śrīgurucaraṇakamalebhyo namaḥ । 11

नैवेद्यम् समर्पयामि श्रीगुरुचरणकमलेभ्यः नमः ।

नैवेद्यम् n2/1 food समर्पयामि लट् i/1 i heartily offer श्री-गुरु-चरण-कमलेभ्यः m4/3 to exalted master's lotus-like feet

नमः n2/1 humble obeisance

नैवेद्यम् from नि + विद् ।

11.

Food to nourish the soul. Food to guide the brain. Food to satisfy the heart. Food to make friends.

We generally offer sattvic foods like fruits, nuts, kheer. However whatever one likes, one may offer...

Three types of fruits may be offered, to suit various palates (sour, sweet, thick).

It also means that we are attending to the three gunas in the body and mind. We are eating a balanced diet to keep our tri-dosha in check.

Remember that some foods make the tongue happy, while others are conducive for the stomach. Be balanced, be choosy and caring to suit yourself and your fitness.

Keep in mind that seasonal foods will get naturally digested, while esoteric or out-of-season foods of faraway lands might make one weak and itchy.

12th Enjoyable Drink to cement the Union

आचमनीयं समर्पयामि श्रीगुरुचरणकमलेभ्यो नमः । १२
ācamanīyaṃ
samarpayāmi śrīgurucaraṇakamalebhyo namaḥ I 12

आचमनीयम् समर्पयामि श्रीगुरुचरणकमलेभ्यः नमः ।

आचमनीयम् n2/1 water for sipping समर्पयामि लट् i/1 i heartily offer श्री-गुरु-चरण-कमलेभ्यः m4/3 to exalted master's lotus-like feet नमः n2/1 humble obeisance

12.

A drink at the end to wash down the food is highly recommended.

Normally we begin our meals with a soup or a juice. At the end too we may sip some honeyed water काढ़ा, or a single sip of plain water to clear the morsels from the mouth and feel fresh.

It is a tradition in some cultures to sip a hot drink a short while post meals.

13th Strength check and restore

ताम्बूलं समर्पयामि श्रीगुरुचरणकमलेभ्यो नमः । १३
tāmbūlaṃ
samarpayāmi śrīgurucaraṇakamalebhyo namaḥ । 13

ताम्बूलम् समर्पयामि श्रीगुरुचरणकमलेभ्यः नमः ।

ताम्बूलम् n2/1 betel nut and leaf समर्पयामि लट् i/1 i heartily offer श्री-गुरु-चरण-कमलेभ्यः m4/3 to exalted master's lotus-like feet नमः n2/1 humble obeisance

13.

A betel nut and two betel leaves are now presented.

Betel leaf helps to clear the throat and tongue. The betel nut helps to check tooth firmness and allows us to take corrective measures if needed in the dental department.

The people of yore ensured that our meal itself would point out deficiences in our health if any, so that we would not delay taking appropriate measures to ensure soundness of the body.

14th Humility preserve

श्रीफलं समर्पयामि श्रीगुरुचरणकमलेभ्यो नमः । १४

śrīphalaṃ

samarpayāmi śrīgurucaraṇakamalebhyo namaḥ । 14

श्रीफलम् समर्पयामि श्रीगुरुचरणकमलेभ्यः नमः ।

श्रीफलम् $^{n2/1}$ coconut समर्पयामि $^{लट् \, i/1}$ i heartily offer श्री-

गुरु-चरण-कमलेभ्यः $^{m4/3}$ to exalted master's lotus-like feet

नमः $^{n2/1}$ humble obeisance

14.

We offer a whole coconut. It is of the ripe variety, with a brown hairy shell, white kernel, and delicious water.

Coconut represents our body, brain, and ego. It shows us how we must behave or be.

- A hard shell to fend off challenges and have high immunity to prevent seasonal illness
- Well groomed hair to look handsome
- White kernel fruit to imply a clarity in thinking and decision-making and a purity in intention
- Delicious water to show a loving heart, an easy friendliness, and a melted ego

In other words, a fitness and an attitude that the Lord would be very proud of.

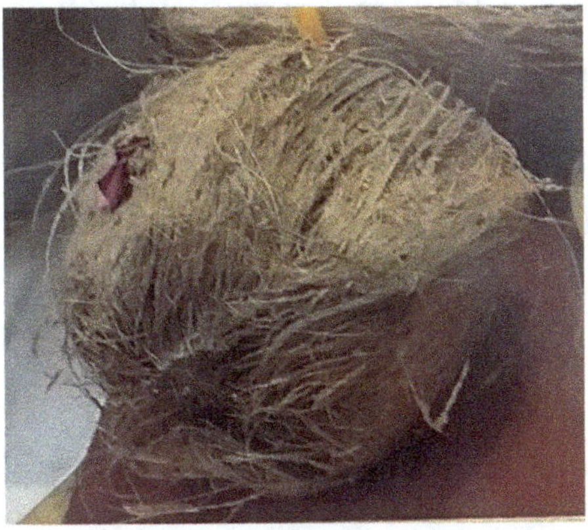

Aarti - Lamps

<u>आरार्तिक्यम्</u>

कर्पूरगौरं करुणावतारं संसारसारं भुजगेन्द्रहारम् ।
सदावसन्तं हृदयारविन्दे भवं भवानीसहितं नमामि ॥

<u>ārārtikyam</u>

karpūragauraṃ karuṇāvatāraṃ saṃsārasāraṃ bhujagendrahāram | sadāvasantaṃ hṛdayāravinde bhavaṃ bhavānīsahitaṃ namāmi ||

कर्पूरगौरम् करुणावतारम् संसारसारम् भुजगेन्द्रहारम् ।
सदावसन्तम् हृदयारविन्दे भवम् भवानीसहितम् नमामि ॥

कर्पूर-गौरम् n2/1 adj camphor like creamy white करुणा-अवतारम् m2/1 compassion incarnate संसार-सारम् m2/1 society and relationship's essence भुजगेन्द्र-हारम् m2/1 adorned by the Serpent King as a garland । सदा-वसन्तम् m2/1 perpetual spring season हृदया-अरविन्दे n7/1 in the heart's lotus भवम् m2/1 deeply connected to emotion i.e. Lord Shiva भवानी-सहितम् m2/1 upholding all material and dependent forms i.e. with Mother नमामि लट् i/1 i wish to follow in entirety ॥

विन्दे from 1450. विद् विचारणे । 7cA, अरविन्द = white lotus. Note: Serpent King is a metaphor in Sanskrit literature to denote all terrible, cruel, destructive energies.

∞.

Lamps are that which radiate joy and happiness and spread good cheer far and wide.

We light a camphor lamp to be grateful for the Sun in our lives. The sun and the moon complement each other, and the moon has many stars in tow. Some healing, some aggravating, but all guiding us towards a highly creative, productive, sincere effort filled living.

An Aarti plate is done in a very special manner. We use a natural metal like copper, brass, or silver. We decorate the edges with multicolored fragrant flowers.

We draw a Swastika with red kumkum powder in the middle and put a heap of rice there. On that we place a lamp (of brass or copper or silver), filled with ghee or clarified butter, and a cotton wick.

Upon that we place a piece of natural camphor, and light it while singing the hymns, and moving the plate in large clockwise circles.

The camphor evaporates away quickly without leaving any residue behind, such should be our intention and action. The ghee lamp thereafter gets lit and shines brightly for a long time. Such should be one's habits, body tone, and status in society.

15th Offer Everything

आरार्तिक्यं समर्पयामि श्रीगुरुचरणकमलेभ्यो नमः । १५
ārārtikyaṃ
samarpayāmi śrīgurucaraṇakamalebhyo namaḥ I 15

आरार्तिक्यम् समर्पयामि श्रीगुरुचरणकमलेभ्यः नमः ।

आरार्तिक्यम् $^{n2/1}$ camphor lamp समर्पयामि $^{लट् i/1}$ i heartily offer श्री-गुरु-चरण-कमलेभ्यः $^{m4/3}$ to exalted master's lotus-like feet नमः $^{n2/1}$ humble obeisance

Offer Intimacy

आचमनीयं समर्पयामि श्रीगुरुचरणकमलेभ्यो नमः ॥
ācamanīyaṃ
samarpayāmi śrīgurucaraṇakamalebhyo namaḥ II

आचमनीयम् समर्पयामि श्रीगुरुचरणकमलेभ्यः नमः ॥

आचमनीयम् $^{n2/1}$ water for sprinkling समर्पयामि $^{लट् i/1}$ i heartily offer श्री-गुरु-चरण-कमलेभ्यः $^{m4/3}$ to exalted master's lotus-like feet नमः $^{n2/1}$ humble obeisance

15.

We gently place the Aarti plate on the ground, in a place wherein the light is visible to all.

We have offered everything; we have surrendered our mind and body, heart and soul, to the Guru. We submit to the Guru with a pleasant abandon. Now that he has our cares, we become carefree.

O.

We observe our mind and see if we can feel a oneness. We become One with it all.

No more quarrels, no more bitterness, no more shouting within the family. No more waking up with a guilt, all our fears have evaporated.

It is a freedom of the highest order.

Gratefulness – Flowers

<u>पुष्पाञ्जलिम्</u>

गुरुर्ब्रह्मा गुरुर्विष्णुः गुरुर्देवो महेश्वरः ।

गुरुस्साक्षात् परंब्रह्म तस्मै श्रीगुरवे नमः ॥ १

puṣpāñjalim

gururbrahmā gururviṣṇuḥ gururdevo maheśvaraḥ I

gurussākṣāt paraṃbrahma tasmai śrīgurave namaḥ II 1

गुरुः ब्रह्मा गुरुः विष्णुः गुरुः देवः महेश्वरः ।

गुरुः साक्षात् परम् ब्रह्म तस्मै श्रीगुरवे नमः ॥

गुरुः [m1/1] the Preceptor ब्रह्मा [m1/1] Brahma गुरुः [m1/1] the Master विष्णुः [m1/1] Vishnu गुरुः [m1/1] the Guru देवः [m1/1] Light महेश्वरः [m1/1] Maheshwar i.e. Shiva I गुरुः [m1/1] the teacher साक्षात् [0] obviously परम् [n1/1 adj] highest ब्रह्म [n1/1] Brahman तस्मै [m4/1 adj] to him श्रीगुरवे [m4/1] to exalted master नमः [n2/1] humble obeisance II

1.

Here we sing praises, and hymns

- to the gathering and the Guru, and
- to the ambience, and the weather.

We invoke the Brahma aspect or the Creator within us, and in the surroundings, and in the Guru.

We invoke the Vishnu aspect or the Sustainer within us, and in the surroundings, and in the Guru.

We invoke the Shiva aspect or the Transformer within us, and in the surroundings, and in the Guru.

We equate the Guru with the act of creating all joys and success and prosperity in our life.

We shoulder Him with the responsibility of maintaining and preserving all we own and all we need; health, wealth and status.

We request of Him to loosen and transform our quirky ways and sordid habits. We need Him to destroy our weaknesses and fears, enemies and the like. We wish that He transforms our children into mature adults and noble citizens.

We sing that our Guru is the direct personification of the great Lord, the highest power in the Universe, and **we gladly agree to His bidding and His directive**.

Acknowledge the Space

अखण्डमण्डलाकारं व्याप्तं येन चराचरम् ।
तत्पदं दर्शितं येन तस्मै श्रीगुरवे नमः ॥ २

akhaṇḍamaṇḍalākāraṃ vyāptaṃ yena carācaram I
tatpadaṃ darśitaṃ yena tasmai śrīgurave namaḥ II 2

अखण्डमण्डलाकारम् व्याप्तम् येन चराचरम् ।
तत्पदम् दर्शितम् येन तस्मै श्रीगुरवे नमः ॥

अखण्ड-मण्डल-आकारम् m2/1 undamaged/uncorrupted detailed and complex figure व्याप्तम् m2/1 adj pervaded everywhere येन m3/1 by whom चर-अचरम् m2/1 adj mobile-immobile I तत्पदम् n2/1 that word दर्शितम् n2/1 adj illumined येन m3/1 by whom तस्मै m4/1 adj to him श्रीगुरवे m4/1 to exalted master नमः n2/1 humble obeisance II

2.

We eulogize that our Master is spotless and stainless.

We acknowledge his detailed makeup and complexity and seriousness of manner, and we ensure not to step on his toes.

We observe that his aura pervades the entire hall, all are showered by his loving presence. He enhances the men and also the furniture. He raises hopes and also elevates the space. Even nature feels happy, flowers bloom, the breeze stirs.

His spoken word shows us the correct way, answers our question in entirety.

Even his unspoken silence melts our confusion away.

To such a benevolent Master, I pray with all my heart.

Acknowledge the Wisdom

श्री ब्रह्मानन्दं परमसुखदं केवलं ज्ञानमूर्तिम् ।
विश्वातीतं गगनसदृशं तत्त्वमस्यादि लक्ष्यम् ॥ ३

śrī brahmānandaṃ paramasukhadaṃ kevalaṃ jñānamūrtim I viśvātītaṃ gaganasadṛśaṃ tattvamasyādi lakṣyam II 3

श्री ब्रह्मानन्दम् परमसुखदम् केवलम् ज्ञानमूर्तिम् ।
विश्वातीतम् गगनसदृशम् तत् त्वम् असि आदि लक्ष्यम् ॥

श्री 0 glorious (title) ब्रह्म-आनन्दम् m2/1 to the Brahmi bliss परम-सुखदम् m2/1 adj to the ultimate joy केवलम् 0 adv only ज्ञान-मूर्तिम् m2/1 to the personification of knowledge I विश्व-अतीतम् m2/1 adj to the one who is beyond the world i.e. transcendent गगन-सदृशम् m2/1 adj to the one who is space-like i.e. massive infinite तत् n2/1 that (Lord) त्वम् n2/1 you असि n2/1 are आदि 0 the primal लक्ष्यम् n2/1 the aim II

तत् त्वम् असि = तत्त्वमसि । a Mahavakya from the Chandogya Upanishad verse 6.8.7 of Samaveda.
असि from 1065. अस् भुवि । 2cP

3.

We further eulogize the Guru in glowing terms.

We say:
Brahmanandam = his state is full of Brahmi bliss, bubbling joy, perfect cheerfulness, radiating contentment.
Paramsukhadam = he enjoys the highest level of comforts. Being comfortable does not depend solely on wealth and resources. It additionally entails a pleasant state of mind and a fit body. Many rich elite people we see, they have huge homes, expensive cars and mobile phones; but their body is out of shape, their kids are not in control, they are angered because their brother or someone seems to have more wealth. In fact they also have cash, but they do not spend it wisely, being of a miserly and suspicious nature.
Jnanamurtim = he is an embodiment of knowledge, wisdom, talent. He can handle difficult challenges, can solve tricky problems, even superstars seek his help.
Vishvatitam = he lives beyond the worldy trials and tribulations. The thorny relationships, society goings-on, terrible news headlines, stormy upheavels; none of it touches him, nothing injures him.
Gagansadrisham = he is infinite like the space, he is massive like the clear open skies, his temperament doesn't get clouded, events do not leave damaging impressions on him, people worries do no bother.
Tattvamasi = that thou art. That you are. He is the Lord. He is that *known as* Brahman. He is the Truth.
Adi Lakshyam = he is my main motive, my primal aim, my sole goal, my all in all.

Acknowledge the Purity

एकं नित्यं विमलमचलं सर्वधीसाक्षिभूतम् ।
भावातीतं त्रिगुणसहितं सद्गुरुं तं नमामि ॥ ४

ekaṃ nityaṃ vimalamacalaṃ sarvadhīsākṣibhūtam I
bhāvātītaṃ triguṇasahitaṃ sadguruṃ taṃ namāmi II 4

एकम् नित्यम् विमलम् अचलम् सर्वधीसाक्षिभूतम् ।
भावातीतम् त्रिगुणसहितम् सद्गुरुम् तम् नमामि ॥

एकम्[m2/1 adj] to the one नित्यम्[m2/1 adj] to the eternal constant वि-मलम्[m2/1 adj] devoid of impurity अ-चलम्[m2/1 adj] non-wavering सर्व-धी-साक्षि-भूतम्[m2/1] to the one who witnesses the thoughts of all beings I भाव-अतीतम्[m2/1 adj] beyond emotional turbulence/blackmail त्रि-गुण-सहितम्[m2/1 adj] with the triCreativeEnergies of Sattva Rajas Tamas सद्-गुरुम्[m2/1] to the true Master तम्[m2/1] to him नमामि[लट् i/1] my whole being expresses grateful surrender II

त्रिगुणरहितम् was modified to त्रिगुणसहितम् by Gurudev in our Guru Puja class, who said "रहितम् is used for one without physical body, while सहितम् is used for one presently in physical body".

4.

Praising is a divine quality. Just as abuse makes us feel dull and bitter, praise makes us feel cheerful and well. When we praise the Guru, we are not just praising someone else. Infact the words of praise come back to us manifold and heal us, help us in numerous ways.

We continue by singing:

Ekam = his state is of Oneness with the Divine
Nityam = his peace is perpetual, lasting, unbroken
Vimalam = his mind is clean, his thoughts are pure
Achalam = his emotions are unfluctuating
Sarvadhisakshibhutam = his state is full of Brahmi,
Bhavatitam = his heart is beyond influence of storms
Trigunasahitam = he maintains a balance of tridosha

Sadguru tam namami = O True Master! My soul merges, gets absorbed in thee.

Acknowledge the Body

अज्ञानतिमिरान्धस्य ज्ञानाञ्जनशलाकया ।
चक्षुरुन्मीलितं येन तस्मै श्री गुरवे नमः ॥ ५

ajñānatimirāndhasya jñānāñjanaśalākayā ǀ
cakṣurunmīlitaṃ yena tasmai śrī gurave namaḥ ǁ 5

अज्ञानतिमिरान्धस्य ज्ञानाञ्जनशलाकया ।
चक्षुः उन्मीलितम् येन तस्मै श्री गुरवे नमः ॥

अज्ञान-तिमिर-अन्धस्य [m6/1 adj] of ignorance *that is* densely blinding ज्ञान-अञ्जन-शलाकया [f3/1] dusted by probe of self-enquiry । चक्षुः [n2/1] eye उन्मीलितम् [n2/1 adj] well-opened येन [m3/1] by whom तस्मै [m4/1 adj] to him श्रीगुरवे [m4/1] to exalted master नमः [n2/1] humble obeisance ॥

5.

We end with the priceless benefits we **receive** from his Satsang and company:

He has removed my shackles in the form of deep veil of maya.

He has given me the technique of Self-enquiry and Meditation to keep my brain functional and my heart intact and pure.

He has given me a perfect vision to move forward in life, grow rich in success, and expand my horizon tremendously.

I touch his hallowed feet.

16th Drop yourSelf

पुष्पाञ्जलिं समर्पयामि श्री श्री गुरुचरणकमलेभ्यो नमः । १६
puṣpāñjaliṃ
samarpayāmi śrī śrī gurucaraṇakamalebhyo namaḥ I 16

पुष्पाञ्जलिम् समर्पयामि श्री श्री गुरुचरणकमलेभ्यः नमः ।

पुष्प-अञ्जलिम् n2/1 a flower with open palms समर्पयामि लट् i/1 i heartily offer श्री श्री गुरु-चरण-कमलेभ्यः m4/3 at my exalted master Sri Sri Ravi Shankar's lotus-like feet नमः n2/1 humble obesiance

श्री श्री = here we take it to mean Sri Sri Ravi Shankar, but you are free to use it to reference your own beloved preceptor.
Note: the original text has श्री once.

16.

Finally, we offer ourselves in the form of our Ego or limited identity.

We offer the deepest corner of our heart. We offer all that bothers us and we offer all that pleases us.

We feel free and alive.
We give a bright smile.

Our eyes are twinkling.
Our hopes are within reach.
Our aims are achieved.

Silence

Just let go and be deeply absorbed in silent stillness for some moments.

जय गुरुदेव

Bhajan – Singing

गुरुदेव गुरु ॐ , नमः शिवाय ।
गुरुदेव गुरु ॐ , नमः शिवाय । chorus

नमः शिवाय , नमः शिवाय शिवः ।
नमः शिवाय , नमः शिवाय शिवः । chorus

नमः शिवाय , नमः शिवाय शिवः ।
नमः शिवाय , नमः शिवाय शिवः । chorus

गुरु ॐ जय जय सद्गुरुः ।
गुरु ॐ जय जय सद्गुरुः । chorus

शिव ॐ जय जय सदाशिवः ।
शिव ॐ जय जय सदाशिवः । chorus

गुरुदेव गुरु ॐ , नमः शिवाय ।
गुरुदेव गुरु ॐ , नमः शिवाय । chorus repeat and fade

Gurudev Guru Om, Namah Shivaya
Gurudev Guru Om, Namah Shivaya

Namah Shivaya, Namah Shivaya Shiva
Namah Shivaya, Namah Shivaya Shiva

Namah Shivaya, Namah Shivaya Shiva
Namah Shivaya, Namah Shivaya Shiva

Guru Om, Jaya Jaya Sadguru
Guru Om, Jaya Jaya Sadguru

Shiva Om, Jaya Jaya Sada Shiva
Shiva Om, Jaya Jaya Sada Shiva

Gurudev Guru Om, Namah Shivaya
Gurudev Guru Om, Namah Shivaya

Latin Transliteration Chart

International Alphabet of Sanskrit Transliteration (I.A.S.T.)

a	ā	i	ī	u	ū	ṛ	ṝ	ḷ	
अ	आ	इ	ई	उ	ऊ	ऋ	ॠ	ऌ	
						◌ृ	◌ॄ	◌ॢ	
e	ai	o	au	ṃ	m̐	ḥ	Ardha Visarga	oṃ	
ए	ऐ	ओ	औ	◌ं	◌ँ	◌ः	◌ᳲ	ॐ	
Consonants shown with vowel 'a= अ' for uttering									
ka	क	ca	च	ṭa	ट	ta	त	pa	प
kha	ख	cha	छ	ṭha	ठ	tha	थ	pha	फ
ga	ग	ja	ज	ḍa	ड	da	द	ba	ब
gha	घ	jha	झ	ḍha	ढ	dha	ध	bha	भ
ṅa	ङ	ña	ञ	ṇa	ण	na	न	ma	म
ya	ra	la	va		ḷa	'			
य	र	ल	व		ळ	ऽ			
					Consonant only				
śa	ṣa	sa	ha		ka	क्अ = क			
श	ष	स	ह		k	क्			

Verses for Chanting

॥ गुरु पूजा ॥

सदाशिवसमारम्भां शङ्कराचार्यमध्यमाम् ।
अस्मद् श्रीगुरुपर्यन्तां वन्दे गुरुपरम्पराम् ॥ १

अपवित्रः पवित्रो वा सर्वावस्थाङ्गतोऽपि वा ।
यस्स्मरेत् पुण्डरीकाक्षं स बाह्याभ्यन्तरः शुचिः ॥ २

नारायणं पद्मभवं वशिष्ठं शक्तिञ्च तत्पुत्रपराशरञ्च ।
व्यासं शुकं गौडपदं महान्तं गोविन्दयोगीन्द्रमथास्य शिष्यम् ॥ ३

श्री शङ्कराचार्यमथास्य पद्मपादञ्च हस्तामलकञ्च शिष्यम् ।
तं त्रोटकं वार्त्तिककारमन्यान् अस्मद् गुरून् सन्ततमानतोऽस्मि ॥
४

श्रुतिस्मृतिपुराणानाम् आलयं करुणालयम् ।
नमामि भगवत्पादं शङ्करं लोकशङ्करम् ॥ ५

शङ्करं शङ्कराचार्यं केशवं बादरायणम् ।
सूत्रभाष्यकृतौ वन्दे भगवन्तौ पुनः पुनः ॥ ६

यद्द्वारे निखिला निलिम्पपरिषद् सिद्धिं विधत्तेऽनिशम् ।
श्रीमच्छ्रीलसितं जगद्गुरुपदं नत्वात्मतृप्तिङ्गताः ॥ ७

लोकाज्ञानपयोदपाटनधुरं श्री शङ्करं शर्मदम् ।
ब्रह्मानन्दसरस्वतीं गुरुवरं ध्यायामि ज्योतिर्मयम् ॥ ८

आवाहनं समर्पयामि श्रीगुरुचरणकमलेभ्यो नमः । १
आसनं समर्पयामि श्रीगुरुचरणकमलेभ्यो नमः । २
स्नानं समर्पयामि श्रीगुरुचरणकमलेभ्यो नमः । ३
वस्त्रं समर्पयामि श्रीगुरुचरणकमलेभ्यो नमः । ४
चन्दनं समर्पयामि श्रीगुरुचरणकमलेभ्यो नमः । ५
अक्षतान् समर्पयामि श्रीगुरुचरणकमलेभ्यो नमः । ६
पुष्पं समर्पयामि श्रीगुरुचरणकमलेभ्यो नमः । ७
धूपं समर्पयामि श्रीगुरुचरणकमलेभ्यो नमः । ८
दीपं समर्पयामि श्रीगुरुचरणकमलेभ्यो नमः । ९
आचमनीयं समर्पयामि श्रीगुरुचरणकमलेभ्यो नमः । १०
नैवेद्यं समर्पयामि श्रीगुरुचरणकमलेभ्यो नमः । ११
आचमनीयं समर्पयामि श्रीगुरुचरणकमलेभ्यो नमः । १२
ताम्बूलं समर्पयामि श्रीगुरुचरणकमलेभ्यो नमः । १३
श्रीफलं समर्पयामि श्रीगुरुचरणकमलेभ्यो नमः । १४

आरार्तिक्यम्

कर्पूरगौरं करुणावतारं संसारसारं भुजगेन्द्रहारम् ।
सदावसन्तं हृदयारविन्दे भवं भवानीसहितं नमामि ॥
आरार्तिक्यं समर्पयामि श्रीगुरुचरणकमलेभ्यो नमः ।
आचमनीयं समर्पयामि श्रीगुरुचरणकमलेभ्यो नमः ॥ १५

पुष्पाञ्जलिम्

गुरुर्ब्रह्मा गुरुर्विष्णुः गुरुर्देवो महेश्वरः ।
गुरुस्साक्षात् परंब्रह्म तस्मै श्रीगुरवे नमः ॥ १

अखण्डमण्डलाकारं व्याप्तं येन चराचरम् ।
तत्पदं दर्शितं येन तस्मै श्रीगुरवे नमः ॥ २

श्री ब्रह्मानन्दं परमसुखदं केवलं ज्ञानमूर्तिम् ।
विश्वातीतं गगनसदृशं तत्त्वमस्यादि लक्ष्यम् ॥ ३

एकं नित्यं विमलमचलं सर्वधीसाक्षिभूतम् ।
भावातीतं त्रिगुणसहितं सद्गुरुं तं नमामि ॥ ४

अज्ञानतिमिरान्धस्य ज्ञानाञ्जनशलाकया ।
चक्षुरुन्मीलितं येन तस्मै श्री गुरवे नमः ॥ ५

पुष्पाञ्जलिं_समर्पयामि श्री श्री गुरुचरणकमलेभ्यो नमः ॥ १६ ॥

Note: No of Verses = 8+2+10+16 = 36.

- Initial Verses for Guru Parampara = 8
- Aarti Verses = 2
- Guru Praise Verses = 10
- Offerings Verses = 16

II guru pūjā II

sadāśivasamārambhāṃ śaṅkarācāryamadhyamām I
asmad śrīguruparyantāṃ vande guruparamparām II 1

apavitraḥ pavitro vā sarvāvasthāṅgato'pi vā I yassmaret
puṇḍarīkākṣaṃ sa bāhyābhyantaraḥ śuciḥ II 2

nārāyaṇaṃ padmabhavaṃ vaśiṣṭhaṃ śaktiñca
tatputraparāśarañca I vyāsaṃ śukaṃ gauḍapadaṃ
mahāntaṃ govindayogīndramathāsya śiṣyam II 3

śrī śaṅkarācāryamathāsya padmapādañca
hastāmalakañca śiṣyam I taṃ troṭakaṃ
vārttikakāramanyān asmad gurūn santatamānato'smi II
4

śrutismṛtipurāṇānām ālayaṃ karuṇālayam I namāmi
bhagavatpādaṃ śaṅkaraṃ lokaśaṅkaram II 5

śaṅkaraṃ śaṅkarācāryaṃ keśavaṃ bādarāyaṇam I
sūtrabhāṣyakṛtau vande bhagavantau puna× punaḥ II 6

yaddvāre nikhilā nilimpapariṣad siddhiṃ vidhatte'niśam
I śrīmacchrīlasitaṃ jagadgurupadaṃ
natvātmatṛptiṅgatāḥ II 7

lokājñānapayodapāṭanadhuraṃ śrī śaṅkaraṃ śarmadaṃ I brahmānandasarasvatīṃ guruvaraṃ dhyāyāmi jyotirmayam II 8

āvāhanaṃ samarpayāmi śrīgurucaraṇakamalebhyo namaḥ I 1
āsanaṃ samarpayāmi śrīgurucaraṇakamalebhyo namaḥ I 2
snānaṃ samarpayāmi śrīgurucaraṇakamalebhyo namaḥ I 3
vastraṃ samarpayāmi śrīgurucaraṇakamalebhyo namaḥ I 4
candanaṃ samarpayāmi śrīgurucaraṇakamalebhyo namaḥ I 5
akṣatān samarpayāmi śrīgurucaraṇakamalebhyo namaḥ I 6
puṣpaṃ samarpayāmi śrīgurucaraṇakamalebhyo namaḥ I 7
dhūpaṃ samarpayāmi śrīgurucaraṇakamalebhyo namaḥ I 8
dīpaṃ samarpayāmi śrīgurucaraṇakamalebhyo namaḥ I 9
ācamanīyaṃ samarpayāmi śrīgurucaraṇakamalebhyo namaḥ I 10
naivedyaṃ samarpayāmi śrīgurucaraṇakamalebhyo namaḥ I 11
ācamanīyaṃ samarpayāmi śrīgurucaraṇakamalebhyo namaḥ I 12

tāmbūlaṃ samarpayāmi śrīgurucaraṇakamalebhyo namaḥ I 13

śrīphalaṃ samarpayāmi śrīgurucaraṇakamalebhyo namaḥ I 14

ārārtikyam

karpūragauraṃ karuṇāvatāraṃ saṃsārasāraṃ bhujagendrahāram I sadāvasantaṃ hṛdayāravinde bhavaṃ bhavānīsahitaṃ namāmi II ārārtikyaṃ samarpayāmi śrīgurucaraṇakamalebhyo namaḥ I ācamanīyaṃ samarpayāmi śrīgurucaraṇakamalebhyo namaḥ II 15

puṣpāñjalim

gururbrahmā gururviṣṇuḥ gururdevo maheśvaraḥ I
gurussākṣāt paraṃbrahma tasmai śrīgurave namaḥ II 1
akhaṇḍamaṇḍalākāraṃ vyāptaṃ yena carācaram I
tatpadaṃ darśitaṃ yena tasmai śrīgurave namaḥ II 2
śrī brahmānandaṃ paramasukhadaṃ kevalaṃ jñānamūrtim I viśvātītaṃ gaganasadṛśaṃ tattvamasyādi lakṣyam II 3
ekaṃ nityaṃ vimalamacalaṃ sarvadhīsākṣibhūtam I
bhāvātītaṃ triguṇasahitaṃ sadguruṃ taṃ namāmi II 4
ajñānatimirāndhasya jñānāñjanaśalākayā I
cakṣurunmīlitaṃ yena tasmai śrī gurave namaḥ II 5
puṣpāñjaliṃ samarpayāmi śrī śrī gurucaraṇakamalebhyo namaḥ II 16 II

Sanskrit Grammar

Sandhis separated word by word पदच्छेद (प०),

and with विभक्ति Cases have been listed.

<u>Abbreviations</u>

Nouns

m masculine, **f** feminine, **n** neuter; **V** vocative

1/1 = vibhakti from 1 to 7/number 1 to 3

adj = adjective, adv = adverb

Indeclinables (uninflected nouns or verbs) **0.**
In Sanskrit the **adverbs** are mostly uninflected.
Adjective follows a Substantive in case and number.

Verbs

iii/1 = person i to iii / number 1 to 3

PPP = Past Participle Passive = क्त

PPA = Past Participle Active = क्तवत्

PrPA = Present Participle Active = शतृ / शानच्

FPA = Future Participle Active = लृट् + शतृ

PoPP = Potential Participle Passive = य, तव्य, अनीयर् (gerundive)

It is a common practice in Sanskrit grammar to use a "hyphen" to indicate compounds.
Compound or समास is frequently encountered in Sanskrit literature. It has a beauty and a brevity.

Since Sanskrit is an inflectional language, the **spelling of the same word** changes as per context or usage. Hence words can be **placed anywhere** in a sentence, as in poetic use, without change in meaning. The matrix shows how.

Verb inflections in Sanskrit – a sample chart

982 गमॢ गतौ – to go, also in the sense of attainment			
Present Tense Active voice लट् कर्त्तरि			
Person/no	singular	dual	plural
Third	गच्छति [iii/1]	गच्छतः [iii/2]	गच्छन्ति [iii/3]
Second	गच्छसि [ii/1]	गच्छथः [ii/2]	गच्छथ [ii/3]
First	गच्छामि [i/1]	गच्छावः [i/2]	गच्छामः [i/3]

Noun declensions in Sanskrit – a sample chart

Masculine stem, vowel अ ending			
(र्–आ–म्–अ) राम [m] Lord's name			
	singular [1]	dual [2]	plural [3]
1 Doer	रामः [1/1]	रामौ [1/2]	रामाः [1/3]
2 Object	रामम् [2/1]	रामौ [2/2]	रामान् [2/3]
3 by	रामेण [3/1]	रामाभ्याम् [3/2]	रामैः [3/3]
4 for	रामाय [4/1]	रामाभ्याम् [4/2]	रामेभ्यः [4/3]
5 from	रामात् [5/1]	रामाभ्याम् [5/2]	रामेभ्यः [5/3]
6 of	रामस्य [6/1]	रामयोः [6/2]	रामाणाम् [6/3]
7 in	रामे [7/1]	रामयोः [7/2]	रामेषु [7/3]
Vocative	हे राम [V/1]	हे रामौ [V/2]	हे रामाः [V/3]

Masculine stem, consonant त् ending

मरुत् m Wind, Breeze, Air			
	singular [1]	dual [2]	plural [3]
1 Doer	मरुत् 1/1	मरुतौ 1/2	मरुतः 1/3
2 Object	मरुतम् 2/1	मरुतौ 2/2	मरुतः 2/3
3 by	मरुता 3/1	मरुद्भ्याम् 3/2	मरुद्भिः 3/3
4 for	मरुते 4/1	मरुद्भ्याम् 4/2	मरुद्भ्यः 4/3
5 from	मरुतः 5/1	मरुद्भ्याम् 5/2	मरुद्भ्यः 5/3
6 of	मरुतः 6/1	मरुतोः 6/2	मरुताम् 6/3
7 in	मरुति 7/1	मरुतोः 7/2	मरुत्सु 7/3
Vocative	हे मरुत् V/1	हे मरुतौ V/2	हे मरुतः V/3

Moods and Tenses in Sanskrit

1	लट्	Present Tense
2	लुङ्	Aorist Past Tense,before from now
3	लङ्	Imperfect Past Tense – before from yesterday onwards
4	लिट्	Perfect Past Tense – distant unseen past
5	लृट्	Simple Future Tense – now onwards
6	लुट्	Periphrastic Future Tense – tomorrow onwards
7	लृङ्	Conditional Mood - if/then, past or future
8	लोट्	Imperative Mood – request
9	विधि०	Potential Mood – order विधिलिङ्
10	आशीर्	Benedictive Mood – blessing आशीर्लिङ् (also used in the sense of a curse)

Conjugation process of Verb

अस्मि [लट् i/1] = I am, I exist. Verse 4

Root 1065 √ असँ भुवि । to be, exist. 2cP

1.3.1 भूवादयो धातवः। असँ = अस्अँ

1.3.2 उपदेशेऽजनुनासिक इत् । 1.3.9 तस्य लोपः। अस्

3.4.69 लः कर्मणि च भावे चाकर्मकेभ्यः। अस्

3.2.123 वर्तमाने लट् । 3.4.77 लस्य । अस् + लँट्

1.3.3 हलन्त्यम् । 1.3.9 तस्य लोपः । अस् + लँ

1.3.2 उपदेशेऽजनुनासिक इत् । 1.3.9 तस्य लोपः । अस् + ल्

3.4.78 तिप्तस्झिसिप्थस्थमिब्वस्मस्

तातांझथासाथांध्वमिड्वहिमहिङ् । Parasmaipada

अस् + मिब्वस्मस्।

we are conjugating first person

1.4.101 तिङस्त्रीणि त्रीणि प्रथममध्यमोत्तमाः ।

1.4.102 तान्येकवचनद्विवचनबहुवचनान्येकशः ।

अस् + मिप् । singular

1.4.107 अस्मद्युत्तमः । known as Uttama Purusha

3.4.113 तिङ्शित्सार्वधातुकम् । अस् + मिप्

3.1.68 कर्तरि शप् । 1.1.61 प्रत्ययस्य लुक्श्लुलुपः ।

2.4.72 अदिप्रभृतिभ्यः शपः । इति शप् लुक् । अस् + मिप्

3.4.113 तिङ्शित्सार्वधातुकम् । अस् + मिप्

1.3.3 हलन्त्यम् । 1.3.9 तस्य लोपः । अस् + मि

= अस्मि [लट् i/1] । I am.

Declension process of Noun

अहम् = I

Stem अस्मद् mfn → अहम् mfn 1/1

1.2.45 अर्थवदधातुरप्रत्ययः प्रातिपदिकम् । ओङ्कार

1.2.46 कृत्तद्धितसमासाश्च । 3.1.1 प्रत्ययः । 3.1.2 परश्च ।

4.1.1 ङ्याप्प्रातिपदिकात्

4.1.2 स्वौजस-
मौट्छष्टाभ्याम्भिस्ङेभ्याम्भ्यस्ङसिभ्याम्भ्यस्ङसोसाम्ङ्योस्सुप् ।

1.4.104 विभक्तिश्च । 1.4.103 सुपः = use one of these vibhakti suffix. अस्मद् + सुँ ।

1.4.22 द्व्येकयोर्द्विवचनैकवचने = singular number taken.
अस्मद् + सुँ 1/1 ।

7.1.28 ङेप्रथमयोरम् । अस्मद् + अम् ।

7.2.90 शेषे लोपः । अस्म + अम् ।

7.2.94 त्वाहौ सौ । 7.2.91 मपर्यन्तस्य । अहअ + अम् ।

6.1.96 अतो गुणे । अह + अम् ।

1.3.4 न विभक्तौ तुस्माः = final मकारः of a Vibhakti is not a tag letter. अह + अम् ।

6.1.107 अमि पूर्वः । अह म् ।

= अहम् mfn1/1 ।

can be used in any gender, Masculine/Feminine/Neuter. First case singular. I. This Me. This Body and Mind.

Class Notes

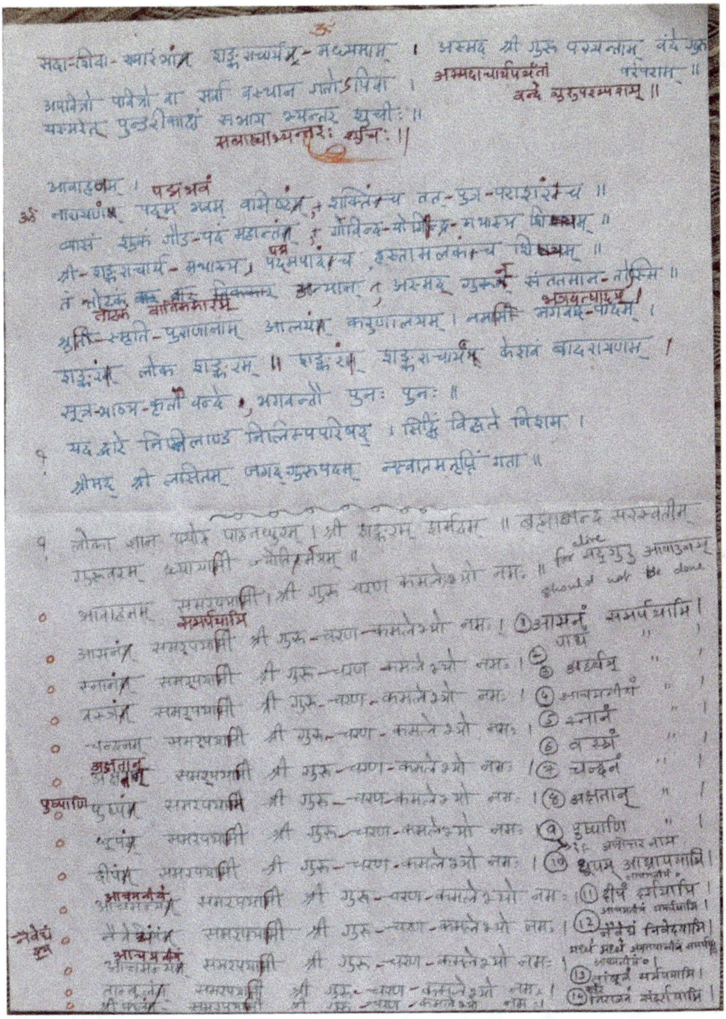

Dated 2 Feb 2016, Vedanta and Sanskrit Gurukul.

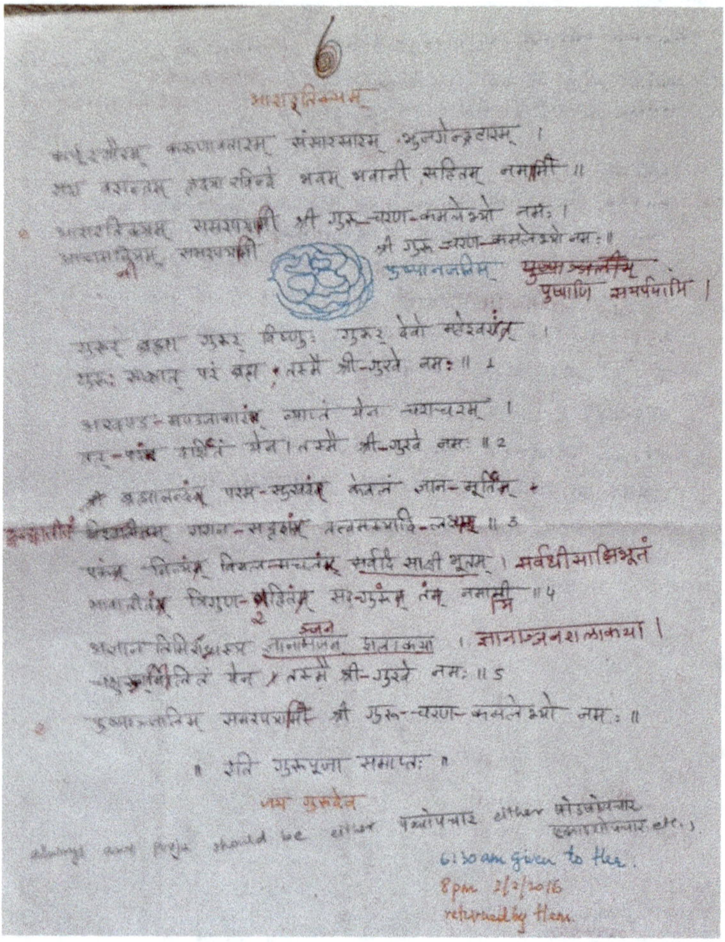

6

आरात्रिक्यम्

कर्पूरगौरम् करुणावतारम् संसारसारम् भुजगेन्द्रहारम् ।
सदा वसन्तम् हृदयारविन्दे भवम् भवानी सहितम् नमामि ॥

आरात्रिक्यम् समर्पयामि श्री गुरु-चरण-कमलेभ्यो नमः ।
आचमनीयम् समर्पयामि श्री गुरु-चरण-कमलेभ्यो नमः ॥
पुष्पाञ्जलिम् पुष्पाञ्जलिम्
पुष्पाणि समर्पयामि ।

गुरुर् ब्रह्मा गुरुर् विष्णुः गुरुर् देवो महेश्वरः ।
गुरुः साक्षात् परं ब्रह्म तस्मै श्री-गुरवे नमः ॥ 1

अखण्ड-मण्डलाकारं व्याप्तं येन चराचरम् ।
तत्-पदं दर्शितं येन । तस्मै श्री-गुरवे नमः ॥ 2

ब्रह्मानन्दं परम-सुखदं केवलं ज्ञान-मूर्तिं
द्वन्द्वातीतं गगन-सदृशं तत्त्वमस्यादि-लक्ष्यम् ॥ 3

एकं नित्यं विमलमचलं सर्वधी साक्षी भूतम् । सर्वधीसाक्षिभूतं
भावातीतं त्रिगुण-रहितं सद्गुरुं तं नमामि ॥ 4

अज्ञान तिमिरान्धस्य ज्ञानाञ्जन शलाकया । ज्ञानाञ्जनशलाकया ।
चक्षुरुन्मीलितं येन तस्मै श्री-गुरवे नमः ॥ 5

पुष्पाञ्जलिम् समर्पयामि श्री गुरु-चरण-कमलेभ्यो नमः ॥

॥ इति गुरुपूजा समाप्तः ॥

जय गुरुदेव

always and puja should be either पञ्चोपचार either षोडशोपचार
द्वादशोपचार etc.)

6:30 am given to Her.
8pm 2/2/2016
returned by Her.

References

https://www.ashtangayoga.info/philosophy/sanskrit-and-devanagari/transliteration-tool/
https://www.learnsanskrit.cc/
https://www.sanskritworld.in/index/Sanskrittool
https://sanskrit.uohyd.ac.in/scl/
https://ashtadhyayi.com/dhatu/
https://www.paulmason.info/gurudev/TMpuja.htm
https://bangaloreashram.org/guru-pooja-phase-1-phase-2/

Guruji performs Puja as Bhanu didi sings July 2011
https://www.youtube.com/watch?v=4QUCp3vnFjA

Guru Puja Group Chanting WCF 2016
https://www.youtube.com/watch?v=TDFSdmk3VBM

Guru Puja by Bhanu didi 2020
https://www.youtube.com/watch?v=g3nFMLsw_Vo

T.R. Chintamani - The Unadi Sutras with the Vritti of Svetavanavasin – 1st – 1992 – Navrang Publishers, New Delhi.

Ashwini Kumar Aggarwal
– Dhatupatha of Panini – 2nd – 2017 –
– Sanskrit Nouns Sabda Manjari – 1st – 2019 –
– Sanskrit Grammar Playful Enquiry – 1st – 2020 –
– Sanskrit Noun Declension using Ashtadhyayi Sutras – 1st – 2022 –
Devotees of Sri Sri Ravi Shankar Ashram, Punjab.

Epilogue

Offer yourSelf. Offer your thoughts emotions desires wants cravings and demands. Offer your likes and dislikes, hate guilt fear pain shame and worry.

Relax and know that the Lord shall address each, all, and everything.

सर्वे भवन्तु सुखिनः । सर्वे सन्तु निरामयाः ।

सर्वे भद्राणि पश्यन्तु । मा कश्चिद् दुःख भाग् भवेत् ॥

ॐ शान्तिः शान्तिः शान्तिः ॥

When faith has blossomed in life,
Every step is led by the Divine.

Sri Sri Ravi Shankar

Om Namah Shivaya

जय गुरुदेव

www.ingramcontent.com/pod-product-compliance
Lightning Source LLC
LaVergne TN
LVHW020426070526
838199LV00004B/294